Oppenheimer: The Father of the Atomic Bomb

James J. Frizzell

All rights reserved. No part of this publication may be reproduced, distributed, or transmitted in any form or by any means, including photocopying, recording, or other electronic or mechanical methods, without the prior written permission of the publisher, except in the case of brief quotations embodied in critical reviews and certain other noncommercial uses permitted by copyright law.

Copyright © James J. Frizzell, 2023.

"Now I am become Death, the destroyer of worlds."

Julius Robert Oppenheimer
1904— 1967

Table of contents:

Chapter 1: Early Years

Chapter 2: Scientific Pioneering

Chapter 3: The Manhattan Project

Chapter 4: The Trinity Test

Chapter 5: The Atomic Bombings of Hiroshima and Nagasaki

Chapter 6: Post-War Advocacy

Chapter 7: The Institute for Advanced Study (IAS)

Chapter 8: Personal Life and Relationships

Chapter 9: Later Years and Legacy, Retirement and Final Years

Chapter 1: Early Years

J. Robert Oppenheimer's journey began on April 22, 1904, in New York City. He was the second child of Julius Oppenheimer and Ella Friedman, both of whom were of German-Jewish descent. The Oppenheimer family was well-educated and financially comfortable, allowing young Robert to grow up in a nurturing and intellectually stimulating environment.

Julius Oppenheimer, his father, was a successful textile importer and owned a prosperous clothing store. He instilled a love of learning and intellectual curiosity in his children, fostering an environment where education was highly valued. Ella, his mother, was a talented artist and introduced Robert to the world of art and culture from an early age.

Robert's elder brother, Frank, would also go on to have a notable career as a physicist and, at times, collaborated with Robert on scientific pursuits. This familial connection played a significant role in shaping Robert's academic interests.

Growing up in an era of rapid scientific advancement and cultural change, young Robert Oppenheimer's early years were marked by a deep fascination with the natural world and a growing enthusiasm for the sciences. His family's support and encouragement would lay the foundation for his future accomplishments in the field of physics, setting the stage for his remarkable journey in the world of science and, eventually, his pivotal role in the development of the atomic bomb.

From a young age, J. Robert Oppenheimer displayed an exceptional aptitude for learning and a keen interest in science. His educational journey was marked by exceptional brilliance and a deep passion for the sciences. His family's emphasis on learning and culture, combined with his innate curiosity, set the stage for his remarkable academic achievements.

Early Education:

Born in 1904 in New York City, Oppenheimer attended the prestigious Ethical Culture Fieldston School. Here, he received a progressive education that encouraged critical thinking and intellectual exploration. It was during these formative years that his fascination with science began to flourish. His early exposure to literature, arts, and science laid a strong foundation for his future academic pursuits.

In 1922, Oppenheimer matriculated at Harvard University, one of the most esteemed institutions in the United States. At Harvard, he continued to stand out academically. Although he explored various subjects, physics and mathematics were his primary interests. Under the mentorship of Percy Bridgman, a Nobel laureate in physics, Oppenheimer conducted research on the compressibility of matter. This research led to his first scientific paper, showcasing his early promise as a physicist.

Doctoral Studies in Europe:

Eager to immerse himself in the vibrant scientific community of Europe, Oppenheimer embarked on a journey that would significantly shape his academic career. He pursued his doctoral studies at some of Europe's most renowned universities:

  - **University of Cambridge:**

Oppenheimer's European journey began at the University of Cambridge, England. Here, he immersed himself in the vibrant scientific community and engaged with brilliant minds. His interactions with Paul Dirac, known for his fundamental contributions to quantum mechanics, left a profound impact on his understanding of the subject. The intellectual rigor and camaraderie at Cambridge broadened his scientific horizons.

- **University of Göttingen:**

Perhaps the most pivotal juncture of Oppenheimer's European education was his tenure at the University of Göttingen in Germany. Under the tutelage of Max Born, a Nobel laureate and eminent physicist, Oppenheimer embarked on research that would shape the course of quantum mechanics. His work on the "Born-Oppenheimer Approximation" laid essential theoretical groundwork for understanding the behavior of molecules, particularly in chemical reactions. This doctoral research culminated in his dissertation and earned him his Ph.D. in 1927.

- University of Leipzig:

Oppenheimer's academic pilgrimage also took him to the University of Leipzig, where he collaborated with another titan of physics, Werner Heisenberg. The insights gained from working with Heisenberg, who would later formulate the famous Uncertainty Principle, further enriched Oppenheimer's understanding of quantum mechanics.

Oppenheimer's time in Europe not only honed his scientific acumen but also exposed him to a diverse array of intellectual influences and cultures, contributing to his unique perspective as a scientist.

Return to the United States:

Armed with a Ph.D. and a wealth of knowledge acquired from Europe's scientific elite, Oppenheimer returned to the United States in 1927. His European education had not only honed his scientific prowess but had also imbued him with a global perspective and a profound understanding of the theoretical underpinnings of quantum mechanics.

Throughout his education, Oppenheimer's brilliance and dedication were evident to his mentors and peers. His journey from a young student at Ethical Culture Fieldston School to a prominent physicist at the forefront of quantum mechanics was marked by a relentless pursuit of knowledge and an unwavering commitment to the scientific endeavor.

Beyond the scientific milieu, Oppenheimer's European experience exposed him to diverse cultures and intellectual traditions. He developed a deep appreciation for art, literature, and philosophy, which would shape his multidisciplinary approach to scientific problems. His fluency in multiple languages, including German and French, facilitated his interactions with fellow scientists and scholars.

These formative years laid the groundwork for his future contributions to the field of physics and, ultimately, his pivotal role in the Manhattan Project.

Chapter 2: Scientific Pioneering

During his formative years in Europe, one of the most pivotal chapters in J. Robert Oppenheimer's academic journey unfolded during his doctoral studies at the University of Göttingen in Germany during the late 1920s. This period significantly contributed to his development as a physicist and would eventually shape his future contributions to quantum mechanics. Let's explore Oppenheimer's experiences during his doctoral studies in Göttingen:

1. **Mentorship Under Max Born:**

Oppenheimer's journey in Göttingen began under the guidance of Max Born, a distinguished physicist and one of the foremost figures in quantum mechanics. Born's insights and pioneering work in the field were instrumental in shaping Oppenheimer's scientific journey.

Born's mentorship provided Oppenheimer with access to cutting-edge research and a profound understanding of quantum theory, which was revolutionizing the world of physics at the time.

2. The "Born-Oppenheimer Approximation":

Oppenheimer's most significant achievement during his time in Göttingen was the development of the "Born-Oppenheimer Approximation," a concept that would become foundational in quantum chemistry and molecular physics.

This approximation, outlined in Oppenheimer's doctoral work, separated the motion of atomic nuclei from that of electrons in molecules. It simplified complex quantum calculations by considering the electronic and nuclear motions as separate problems.

The "Born-Oppenheimer Approximation" allowed scientists to make more manageable calculations when studying molecular structures and chemical reactions. This innovation became a cornerstone in the field of chemistry and significantly advanced our understanding of molecular behavior.

3. Collaborations and Intellectual Exchange:

Göttingen was a hub for scientific activity, attracting brilliant minds from various fields. Oppenheimer's interactions with fellow researchers, such as Werner Heisenberg and Pascual Jordan, enriched his scientific perspectives and broadened his horizons.

These collaborations and intellectual exchanges contributed to the cross-pollination of ideas and played a crucial role in Oppenheimer's growth as a scientist.

4. Doctoral Thesis and Recognition:

In 1927, Oppenheimer successfully defended his doctoral thesis, which centered on the "Born-Oppenheimer Approximation." This work earned him his Ph.D. and garnered recognition within the scientific community.

His thesis was not just a personal achievement; it laid the theoretical groundwork for future research in quantum chemistry and molecular physics. It remains a seminal contribution to these fields and is studied and applied by scientists and researchers worldwide.

5. Legacy:

The "Born-Oppenheimer Approximation" is still a fundamental concept in theoretical chemistry and molecular physics. It is taught in universities and research institutions globally, and its principles are used to model and understand molecular behavior.

Oppenheimer's time in Göttingen, under Max Born's mentorship, solidified his reputation as a brilliant physicist and a creative thinker. His contributions during this period set the stage for his future accomplishments and leadership in the scientific community.

Oppenheimer's doctoral studies in Göttingen were a crucible of scientific innovation. His development of the "Born-Oppenheimer Approximation" not only advanced the field of quantum mechanics but also left an enduring legacy in the study of molecular science, securing his place as one of the most influential physicists of the 20th century.

Contributions to Quantum Mechanics

J. Robert Oppenheimer made significant contributions to the field of quantum mechanics, particularly during his formative years in Europe and his academic career in the United States. Here are some of his key contributions:

1. Born-Oppenheimer Approximation:

Oppenheimer's doctoral research at the University of Göttingen, Germany, led to the development of the "Born-Oppenheimer Approximation." This approximation is a foundational concept in quantum mechanics, particularly in the field of molecular physics and chemistry.

The Born-Oppenheimer Approximation separates the motion of atomic nuclei from that of electrons in molecules. It simplifies complex quantum calculations by treating the electronic and nuclear motions as separate problems.

This approximation is essential for understanding molecular structures, electronic energy levels, and chemical reactions. It enables scientists to make accurate predictions about molecular behavior, contributing significantly to the study of chemistry.

2. Quantum Electrodynamics (QED):

Oppenheimer made noteworthy contributions to quantum electrodynamics, a branch of quantum mechanics that deals with the interaction between matter and electromagnetic radiation.
His work on QED involved studying the behavior of electrons in the presence of

electromagnetic fields, including the emission and absorption of photons.

While his contributions in this area may not be as famous as those of other physicists like Richard Feynman and Julian Schwinger, Oppenheimer's work laid the groundwork for future developments in quantum field theory.

3. Fermi-Thomas Theory:

In collaboration with physicist Enrico Fermi, Oppenheimer contributed to the development of the Fermi-Thomas theory, which describes the behavior of electrons in metals.

This theory provides insights into the electrical conductivity of materials at low temperatures and plays a role in advancing our understanding of condensed matter physics.

4. Oppenheimer-Phillips Process:

Oppenheimer's work extended beyond quantum mechanics to nuclear physics. He collaborated with Melba Phillips to propose the "Oppenheimer-Phillips process," which explains certain nuclear reactions involving proton-proton collisions.

This process is relevant in astrophysics, as it describes a mechanism for the production of deuterium (a heavy isotope of hydrogen) in stellar interiors.

5. Leadership in Theoretical Physics:

While not a specific contribution, Oppenheimer's leadership and mentorship in theoretical physics were instrumental in advancing the field. He trained and influenced numerous physicists who went on to make their own significant contributions to quantum mechanics and related disciplines.

Overall, J. Robert Oppenheimer's contributions to quantum mechanics were multifaceted and impactful. His work in developing the Born-Oppenheimer Approximation, his contributions to quantum electrodynamics and nuclear physics, and his leadership in the scientific community all left an enduring legacy in the field of theoretical physics.

Chapter 3: The Manhattan Project

The Manhattan Project was a top-secret research and development initiative during World War II that led to the creation of the first atomic bombs. This monumental scientific effort was named after the Manhattan Engineer District of the U.S. Army Corps of Engineers, which oversaw the project. Here's a detailed overview of the Manhattan Project:

1. Origins and Motivation:

The origins of the Manhattan Project can be traced back to concerns within the scientific community about the potential for Nazi Germany to develop atomic weapons. In 1939, as World War II loomed, a group of scientists, including Hungarian physicist

Leo Szilard and Italian physicist Enrico Fermi, became increasingly concerned about Nazi Germany's potential development of atomic weapons.

In response to these concerns, President Franklin D. Roosevelt authorized the establishment of the Advisory Committee on Uranium in 1939, which marked the beginning of what would become the Manhattan Project.

2. Key Scientists and Leaders:

To assess the prospects of such a project, the Advisory Committee on Uranium sought out prominent scientists. Among these scientists was J. Robert Oppenheimer, who was already recognized for his outstanding contributions to theoretical physics.

The project's leaders recognized the need for top scientific talent to tackle the complex challenges of developing atomic weapons.

Physicists who had already made significant contributions to the field were sought after. J. Robert Oppenheimer, known for his work in theoretical physics, was appointed as the scientific director due to his exceptional knowledge and leadership qualities.

The Manhattan Project brought together a remarkable assembly of scientists, engineers, and military leaders. Notable figures included J. Robert Oppenheimer, who served as the scientific director, and General Leslie Groves, who oversaw the project's administration.

3. Security and Secrecy:

To ensure the utmost secrecy, participants in the Manhattan Project were told very little about the overall purpose of their work. They were often informed that they were contributing to the war effort without being aware of the specific nature of their research.

Security clearances and background checks were conducted to ensure the trustworthiness of project personnel.

4. Scientific Efforts:

The project had three primary research and development sites:

- **Los Alamos, New Mexico:**

The primary laboratory for theoretical research and bomb design was located in Los Alamos, New Mexico. Oppenheimer, as the director of Los Alamos, played a pivotal role in assembling and leading the team of scientists.

The Los Alamos team worked intensively to develop the design and testing of the atomic bombs.

- **Oak Ridge, Tennessee:**

In Oak Ridge, Tennessee, and Hanford, Washington, scientists and engineers focused on uranium enrichment and plutonium production, respectively. These sites played essential roles in providing the fissile material for the bombs.

- **Hanford, Washington:**

Hanford was responsible for producing plutonium through nuclear reactors, which would serve as the fissile material for another type of atomic bomb.

5. The Bomb Designs:

The Manhattan Project developed two types of atomic bombs:

Little Boy: This bomb used uranium-235 and was dropped on Hiroshima, Japan, on August 6, 1945.
Fat Man: Fat Man employed plutonium-239 and was detonated over Nagasaki, Japan, on

August 9, 1945. These bombings played a significant role in bringing about the end of World War II.

6. The Trinity Test:

Before the atomic bombs were used in combat, a successful test of their destructive power was conducted. The Trinity test, held on July 16, 1945, in New Mexico, confirmed that the bombs were viable weapons.

7. Ethical and Moral Considerations:

The use of atomic bombs raised profound ethical and moral questions. J. Robert Oppenheimer and other scientists involved in the project grappled with the consequences of their work and advocated for international control of nuclear weapons.

The Manhattan Project fundamentally altered the course of history, marking the dawn of the nuclear age and the beginning of the Cold War. It prompted global efforts to prevent the spread of nuclear weapons and led to the establishment of the United Nations and the development of arms control agreements.

The Manhattan Project remains a symbol of scientific achievement, ethical dilemmas, and the power of human ingenuity. It forever changed the geopolitical landscape and continues to shape discussions on nuclear weapons and international security to this day.

Chapter 4: The Trinity Test

The Trinity Test stands as one of the most momentous events in human history, marking the birth of the atomic age and forever altering the course of warfare and international relations. This historic event took place on July 16, 1945, in the remote Jornada del Muerto desert near Alamogordo, New Mexico, as part of the Manhattan Project—the top-secret U.S. effort to develop the atomic bomb during World War II.

The Trinity Test took place on July 16, 1945, in the Jornada del Muerto desert near Alamogordo, New Mexico, USA. The location was chosen for its remote and sparsely populated surroundings.

The Trinity Test was the culmination of years of scientific research, engineering, and development. Its primary objective was to determine if an atomic bomb, specifically an implosion-type bomb known as "Fat Man," would successfully detonate and achieve the expected explosive yield.

Scientists and military leaders understood the immense destructive potential of atomic weapons, and the test was seen as a critical step in evaluating the feasibility of using them in combat.

The atomic device used in the Trinity Test was referred to as "The Gadget." It was essentially a prototype of the Fat Man bomb that would later be dropped on Nagasaki, Japan.

The Gadget used an implosion design, where conventional explosives surrounded a core of plutonium-239. The goal was to compress the core and achieve supercriticality, leading to a nuclear explosion.

The test required extensive preparations, including the assembly of the bomb, construction of the test tower (a 100-foot steel structure), and the setting up of scientific instruments and monitoring equipment to measure the explosion's characteristics.

The utmost secrecy and security surrounded the Trinity Test. Only a select group of scientists, engineers, and military personnel were aware of its purpose.

Access to the test site was tightly controlled, and security measures were put in place to prevent unauthorized personnel from learning about the atomic bomb's details

The morning of July 16, 1945, was marked by anticipation and tension as the countdown to the test began. Scientists, including J. Robert Oppenheimer and Enrico Fermi, stood at observation points several miles from the test site.

The countdown was followed by a series of delays due to weather concerns and technical issues, increasing the tension and anticipation among the observers.

At 5:29:45 a.m. local time, the Gadget was detonated atop a 100-foot steel test tower. The explosion created an intense flash of light, followed by the iconic mushroom cloud rising into the desert sky.

The Trinity Test was an unequivocal success. The Gadget's explosion released an energy equivalent to approximately 20,000 tons of TNT, and created temperatures hotter than the sun's surface demonstrating the incredible power of nuclear fission.

This successful detonation validated the scientific and engineering principles behind nuclear fission and signaled the beginning of the nuclear age. The success of the Trinity Test marked a turning point in history. It demonstrated the feasibility of atomic weapons and had a profound impact on the course of World War II.

The Trinity Test's legacy is profound. It directly led to the use of atomic bombs on the Japanese cities of Hiroshima and Nagasaki in August 1945, hastening the end of World War II.

It set in motion a new era of international relations, characterized by the Cold War and the arms race between the United States and the Soviet Union. The test also prompted ethical and moral reflections among scientists and policymakers, raising questions about the responsible use of this unprecedented destructive power.

The Trinity Test stands as a testament to human achievement and ingenuity, but it also serves as a stark reminder of the potential consequences of scientific discovery. It forever altered the world's geopolitical landscape and continues to shape discussions on nuclear weapons and international security to this day.

The Trinity Test not only ushered in the nuclear age but also raised profound ethical and moral questions about the use of atomic weapons, which would continue to be debated in the post-war era.

After witnessing the destructive power of the atomic bomb, J. Robert Oppenheimer famously quoted a line from Hindu scripture, the Bhagavad Gita, saying, "Now I have become Death, the destroyer of worlds."

The Impact on Oppenheimer and His Team

The Trinity Test had a profound impact on J. Robert Oppenheimer and his team of scientists, both personally and professionally. Here's how this historic event influenced them:

1. Professional Validation:

The successful detonation of the atomic bomb at the Trinity Test provided professional validation for Oppenheimer and his team. It confirmed that their scientific expertise, innovative design, and tireless efforts had led to the development of a revolutionary and devastating weapon.

2. Realization of the Weapon's Power:

Witnessing the power of the atomic bomb at Trinity had a profound effect on Oppenheimer and his colleagues. They had theorized about its potential, but seeing it in action was an entirely different experience.

Oppenheimer famously quoted a line from the Bhagavad Gita, saying, "Now I have become Death, the destroyer of worlds." This quote reflects the weight of responsibility and the moral dilemmas that came with creating such a destructive force.

3. Ethical and Moral Reflection:

The Trinity Test forced Oppenheimer and many of his colleagues to confront the ethical and moral implications of their work. They were aware that the atomic bomb they had developed could cause immense suffering and death if used in warfare.

Oppenheimer, in particular, became an advocate for responsible control of nuclear weapons and played a role in discussions about arms control and international cooperation.

4. Continued Work on the Manhattan Project:

After the Trinity Test, Oppenheimer and his team continued their work on the Manhattan Project. They were tasked with preparing the atomic bombs "Little Boy" and "Fat Man" for deployment in Japan.

The successful deployment of these bombs on Hiroshima and Nagasaki would hasten the end of World War II.

5. Legacy of Responsibility:

The experience of working on the Manhattan Project, witnessing the Trinity Test, and understanding the consequences of atomic weapons left a lasting sense of responsibility on Oppenheimer and his team.

Many scientists who worked on the project dedicated their post-war careers to advocating for arms control, nuclear disarmament, and the peaceful use of atomic energy.

6. Impact on Scientific Careers:

For many scientists who worked on the Manhattan Project, their involvement influenced the trajectory of their scientific careers. Some continued to work on nuclear physics, while others pursued research in areas related to national security and defense.

7. Cold War Era and International Relations:

The Trinity Test marked the beginning of the Cold War era, with the United States and the Soviet Union engaged in an arms race. The scientists involved in the Manhattan Project found themselves in the midst of this geopolitical tension, with their work influencing international relations for decades to come.

In summary, the Trinity Test had a multifaceted impact on J. Robert Oppenheimer and his team of scientists. While it affirmed their scientific achievements, it also compelled them to grapple with the moral implications of their work and to advocate for responsible control of nuclear weapons. The legacy of their experiences continued to shape their lives and the course of international affairs long after the test's detonation.

Chapter 5: The Atomic Bombings of Hiroshima and Nagasaki

The atomic bombings of Hiroshima and Nagasaki are among the most significant and controversial events in modern history. These bombings, which occurred during World War II, had profound implications for warfare, international relations, and the ethics of using nuclear weapons.

On August 6, 1945, the United States dropped the first atomic bomb, "Little Boy," on the Japanese city of Hiroshima. The bomb exploded approximately 2,000 feet above the city. The explosion released an intense burst of energy, creating a fireball and a powerful shockwave. The city was devastated, with widespread destruction and loss of life.

Just three days later, on August 9, 1945, a second atomic bomb, "Fat Man," was dropped on the city of Nagasaki. This bomb exploded over the Urakami Valley. Nagasaki, like Hiroshima, suffered massive destruction, with tens of thousands of casualties.

The immediate impact of the bombings was catastrophic. Tens of thousands of people died instantly, and many more suffered horrific injuries.

The long-term effects of radiation exposure led to a significant number of deaths in the years that followed, as survivors faced increased risks of cancer and other health issues.

The bombings of Hiroshima and Nagasaki played a pivotal role in bringing about the end of World War II. The devastation and the realization of the power of atomic weapons prompted Japan to surrender on August 15, 1945.

The use of atomic bombs on civilian populations raised profound ethical and moral questions. Some argued that it was a necessary measure to end the war quickly and save lives, given the anticipated casualties of a full-scale invasion of Japan. Others contended that the bombings constituted a horrific act of indiscriminate destruction and a violation of the principles of just warfare.

The atomic bombings marked the beginning of the nuclear age and initiated the Cold War between the United States and the Soviet Union. Both nations embarked on an arms race, developing larger and more powerful nuclear arsenals.

In the aftermath of the bombings, survivors, known as hibakusha, and concerned individuals around the world began advocating for peace and nuclear disarmament. Their efforts contributed to the growing anti-nuclear movement. Hiroshima and Nagasaki have become symbols of the devastating consequences of nuclear warfare. Both cities have established peace parks and museums to remember the victims and promote a message of peace.

The atomic bombings of Hiroshima and Nagasaki left an enduring legacy of caution and concern regarding the use of nuclear weapons. The specter of mutually assured destruction during the Cold War tempered the use of such weapons in subsequent conflicts.

The atomic bombings of Hiroshima and Nagasaki remain subjects of historical debate, ethical reflection, and lessons in the destructive power of nuclear weapons. They serve as a reminder of the importance of pursuing peaceful solutions to conflicts and the imperative of preventing the use of such devastating weapons in the future.

The Decision to Use the Atomic Bomb

The decision to use the atomic bomb during World War II was a complex and controversial one that involved multiple factors and considerations. This decision ultimately fell to U.S. President Harry S. Truman, who had to weigh the moral, military, and strategic implications of using this powerful new weapon. Here's an overview of the key factors that influenced the decision:

1. Ending the War Quickly:

One of the primary arguments in favor of using the atomic bomb was the belief that it would hasten the end of the war. By August 1945, Japan was on the brink of defeat, but its leadership had not yet surrendered. An invasion of Japan was planned, and it was expected to result in massive casualties on both sides.

The proponents of using the bomb argued that it could potentially save lives by forcing Japan's surrender without the need for a full-scale invasion.

2. Potential Casualties of Invasion:

The projected casualties for the invasion of Japan, codenamed Operation Downfall, were estimated to be extremely high. It was believed that hundreds of thousands of Allied soldiers and millions of Japanese civilians could perish in the fighting.

3. Moral and Ethical Considerations:

Opponents of the bomb's use argued that it represented a grave ethical dilemma. Dropping an atomic bomb on a densely populated civilian area could result in the indiscriminate killing of non-combatants, including women and children.

The moral implications of using such a destructive weapon weighed heavily on the decision-makers.

4. The Potsdam Declaration:

Prior to the bombings, the Potsdam Declaration was issued by the Allies in July 1945, calling for Japan's unconditional surrender. Japan did not respond positively, leading to concerns that the war might continue indefinitely.

5. Desire to Show U.S. Strength:

Some argued that using the atomic bomb could demonstrate the United States' immense military power to the world, particularly the Soviet Union. The early stages of the Cold War were already taking shape, and there was a desire to establish American dominance.

6. Fear of Soviet Union Involvement:

There was a growing concern that the Soviet Union might enter the war against Japan, potentially gaining influence in East Asia. Using the atomic bomb before the Soviets could intervene could be seen as a strategic advantage.

7. Testing the New Weapon:

The U.S. had invested significant resources in developing the atomic bomb through the Manhattan Project. There was a desire to test the weapon's effectiveness in a real-world scenario.

8. The Decision to Drop the Bombs:

Ultimately, President Truman, after consulting with his advisors, including Secretary of War Henry Stimson and military leaders, made the decision to drop the atomic bombs on Hiroshima and Nagasaki. On August 6, 1945, "Little Boy" was dropped on Hiroshima, and on August 9, 1945, "Fat Man" was dropped on Nagasaki.

The bombings of Hiroshima and Nagasaki led to Japan's surrender on August 15, 1945. They also marked the beginning of the nuclear age and had far-reaching implications for international relations, arms control, and the moral debate surrounding the use of nuclear weapons.

Chapter 6: Post-War Advocacy

After World War II, J. Robert Oppenheimer became a prominent advocate for international control of nuclear weapons and worked tirelessly to promote disarmament efforts. His post-war advocacy was driven by his deep concerns about the ethical and moral implications of nuclear weapons. Here are key aspects of Oppenheimer's post-war advocacy:

1. United Nations and the Baruch Plan:

In 1946, Oppenheimer played a significant role in advising the United States delegation to the United Nations Atomic Energy Commission. He supported the Baruch Plan, which proposed international control of atomic energy and the elimination of nuclear weapons.

The plan called for the establishment of an international agency to oversee nuclear energy and prevent the proliferation of atomic weapons.

2. Acheson-Lilienthal Report:

Oppenheimer also contributed to the drafting of the Acheson-Lilienthal Report in 1946. This report laid out a framework for international control of atomic energy and the eventual elimination of nuclear weapons.

3. Atoms for Peace:

In 1953, President Dwight D. Eisenhower delivered his "Atoms for Peace" speech at the United Nations General Assembly. Oppenheimer was supportive of this initiative, which aimed to promote the peaceful uses of atomic energy and international cooperation in nuclear technology.

Oppenheimer believed that emphasizing the peaceful applications of atomic energy could help reduce the global tension surrounding nuclear weapons.

4. Opposition to Hydrogen Bomb Testing:

Oppenheimer was among the prominent scientists who expressed concerns about the development and testing of the hydrogen bomb (thermonuclear bomb). He believed that the hydrogen bomb's destructive power was unnecessary and destabilizing.

5. Security Clearance Controversy:

Oppenheimer's advocacy for arms control and his associations with individuals who were considered politically suspect led to his security clearance being revoked in 1954 during the height of the McCarthy era.

This controversy and the hearings that followed had a significant impact on his career and reputation.

6. Later Career and Academic Roles:

Despite the security clearance controversy, Oppenheimer continued his academic career. He served as the director of the Institute for Advanced Study in Princeton, New Jersey, from 1947 to 1966, where he made contributions to theoretical physics.

7. Legacy of Advocacy:

Oppenheimer's advocacy for nuclear disarmament and international control of atomic energy left a lasting legacy. He was a leading voice in the debate over the responsible use of nuclear technology and the prevention of nuclear proliferation.

8. Continuing Influence:

Even after his death in 1967, Oppenheimer's ideas and contributions to arms control continued to influence discussions and policies related to nuclear weapons and non-proliferation.

J. Robert Oppenheimer's post-war advocacy reflected his deep commitment to preventing the further use and spread of nuclear weapons. His contributions to international discussions on nuclear disarmament and his efforts to promote peaceful uses of atomic energy played a significant role in shaping the global dialogue on nuclear policy and arms control.

Oppenheimer's Vision for International Control of Nuclear Weapons

J. Robert Oppenheimer's vision for international control of nuclear weapons was rooted in his profound concerns about the destructive potential of atomic energy and the need to prevent its unbridled use.

Oppenheimer advocated for the complete elimination of nuclear weapons as a long-term goal. He believed that the only way to prevent the catastrophic consequences of nuclear war was to work towards a world without these weapons.

Oppenheimer argued that nuclear weapons should be placed under international control and supervision. He believed that no single nation should have unilateral control over such devastating capabilities.

He supported the idea of creating an international authority or agency responsible for managing and overseeing all aspects of atomic energy, including the disarmament process.

Oppenheimer emphasized the importance of using atomic energy for peaceful purposes, such as generating electricity and advancing scientific research. He believed that focusing on the beneficial aspects of nuclear technology would help build a more constructive international environment.

Oppenheimer was deeply concerned about the spread of nuclear weapons to other nations. He believed that international controls and agreements were essential to prevent the proliferation of atomic arms. His vision included mechanisms for verifying compliance with disarmament agreements and preventing the development of nuclear weapons by non-nuclear states.

Oppenheimer was a vocal critic of the development and testing of the hydrogen bomb (thermonuclear bomb). He believed that the H-bomb's destructive power was excessive and that it could trigger a dangerous arms race. His stance against the H-bomb reflected his commitment to promoting measures that limited the scale and destructive potential of nuclear arsenals.

Throughout his advocacy, Oppenheimer grappled with the ethical and moral implications of nuclear weapons. He felt a profound sense of responsibility for the consequences of his work on the atomic bomb.

His advocacy was driven by a belief that scientists and policymakers had a moral duty to prevent the indiscriminate use of nuclear weapons.

While many of Oppenheimer's specific policy proposals were not fully realized during his lifetime, his ideas and advocacy played a significant role in shaping the global discourse on nuclear disarmament and arms control.

His contributions influenced the negotiation of international agreements, such as the Partial Test Ban Treaty in 1963, which restricted nuclear testing in the atmosphere.

In summary, J. Robert Oppenheimer's vision for international control of nuclear weapons centered on the elimination of these weapons, their responsible management under international supervision, and the peaceful use of atomic energy. His legacy includes his tireless efforts to promote arms control, reduce the risks of nuclear conflict, and uphold ethical principles in the face of the unprecedented destructive power of nuclear technology.

The McCarthy Era and Security Clearance Controversy

The McCarthy Era and J. Robert Oppenheimer's security clearance controversy are significant chapters in American history that intersected with the broader context of Cold War tensions and anti-communist sentiment. Here's an overview of these events:

1. McCarthy Era Background:

The McCarthy Era, named after Senator Joseph McCarthy, refers to the period in the United States during the early 1950s characterized by intense anti-communist hysteria, political persecution, and the search for alleged communist sympathizers within government and society.

The era was fueled by the perceived threat of communism, both domestically and internationally, and the fear of Soviet espionage.

2. Oppenheimer's Role in the Manhattan Project:

J. Robert Oppenheimer's involvement in the development of the atomic bomb during World War II earned him a prominent place in the American scientific community.

However, during the post-war period, Oppenheimer's associations with left-leaning individuals and his past involvement with communist organizations attracted scrutiny.

3. Security Clearance Controversy:

In 1953, during the McCarthy Era, Oppenheimer's security clearance was revoked by the Atomic Energy Commission (AEC). This decision came after a series of hearings and investigations into his past associations and loyalty.

4. Factors Leading to Clearance Revocation:

The decision to revoke Oppenheimer's security clearance was influenced by several factors:

His associations with left-wing activists and intellectuals during the 1930s and 1940s, some of whom were suspected of communist ties.

Concerns about his forthrightness in disclosing these associations during background checks.

Allegations, although unproven, that he had obstructed security investigations.

5. Controversy and Public Debate:

Oppenheimer's clearance revocation generated significant controversy and public debate. Many prominent scientists, including Albert Einstein, spoke out in his defense.

The case underscored the tension between scientific freedom and national security interests.

6. Impact on Oppenheimer:

The loss of security clearance had a profound impact on Oppenheimer's career and reputation. He was effectively barred from working on government-sponsored nuclear projects and was marginalized within the scientific community.

Despite this setback, he continued to contribute to academia and theoretical physics.

7. Later Reassessment:

In 1963, President John F. Kennedy awarded Oppenheimer the Enrico Fermi Award, recognizing his contributions to science.

In subsequent years, there was a reevaluation of his security clearance case, with many acknowledging that his contributions to national security far outweighed any perceived security risks.

8. Legacy and Historical Perspective:

The Oppenheimer security clearance controversy remains a symbol of the excesses and injustices of the McCarthy Era.

In 2014, the U.S. Department of Energy posthumously restored Oppenheimer's security clearance, acknowledging that the revocation had been unjust.

In summary, J. Robert Oppenheimer's security clearance controversy during the

McCarthy Era exemplified the broader atmosphere of suspicion and fear of communism that characterized the period. While his clearance was eventually restored posthumously, the episode serves as a cautionary tale about the intersection of national security, civil liberties, and the scientific community during a time of political turmoil.

Chapter 7: The Institute for Advanced Study (IAS)

The Institute for Advanced Study (IAS) is a renowned academic institution located in Princeton, New Jersey, known for its contributions to advanced research in the fields of mathematics, natural sciences, social sciences, and humanities. Established in 1930, the IAS has played a crucial role in fostering groundbreaking research and facilitating intellectual collaboration. Here are key aspects of the Institute for Advanced Study:

1. Founding and Mission:

The IAS was founded by philanthropists Louis Bamberger and his sister, Caroline Bamberger Fuld. They envisioned it as a place where scholars and researchers could engage in unencumbered, deep, and fundamental research across various disciplines.

The primary mission of the IAS is to encourage and support independent, creative, and interdisciplinary scholarship.

2. Notable Scholars and Faculty:

The IAS has been home to numerous renowned scholars and faculty members. Among its early faculty were luminaries such as Albert Einstein, Kurt Gödel, and John von Neumann.

Over the years, many other distinguished scientists, mathematicians, historians, and social scientists have been affiliated with the Institute.

3. Fields of Study:

The IAS encompasses several schools and research programs, including the School of Mathematics, the School of Natural Sciences, the School of Historical Studies, and the School of Social Science.

These schools host scholars, researchers, and faculty members working on a wide range of topics, from particle physics to history and from mathematical logic to social theory.

4. Interdisciplinary Collaboration:

The IAS is known for fostering interdisciplinary collaboration and intellectual exchange. Scholars from different fields are encouraged to interact, leading to innovative research and insights.

5. Contributions to Science and Scholarship:

The IAS has been associated with numerous breakthroughs in science and scholarship. For example, Albert Einstein developed his theory of general relativity while at the Institute.

Kurt Gödel made significant contributions to mathematical logic, and John von Neumann laid the foundation for modern computing and game theory.

6. Role in Academic Freedom:

The IAS has a tradition of supporting academic freedom, allowing researchers the intellectual space and resources to pursue their work without the constraints of teaching or administrative responsibilities.

7. Public Engagement:

While primarily a research institution, the IAS occasionally hosts public lectures, conferences, and events that aim to engage the broader community in discussions about scientific and scholarly topics.

8. Campus and Facilities:

The IAS is situated on a picturesque campus in Princeton, New Jersey, featuring historic buildings and beautiful landscapes conducive to scholarly pursuits. The Institute provides scholars with access to extensive library resources and research facilities.

9. Legacy and Impact:

The Institute for Advanced Study has had a lasting impact on academia and research, both through the groundbreaking work of its faculty and through the generations of scholars it has supported.

It continues to be a hub for intellectual creativity and a symbol of the pursuit of knowledge.

The Institute for Advanced Study is a distinguished institution that has made significant contributions to various fields of study and scholarship. Its commitment to academic freedom and interdisciplinary collaboration has enabled it to remain at the forefront of advanced research and intellectual exploration.

Directorship and Collaborations

The directorship and collaborations at the Institute for Advanced Study (IAS) have played pivotal roles in shaping the institution's academic environment and its contributions to various fields of study. Here are key aspects of the directorship and collaborations at the IAS:

1. Directorship:

The IAS has had a series of distinguished directors who have guided its mission and scholarly activities. Some notable directors include:

- Abraham Flexner (1930-1939): The founding director of the IAS, Flexner played a key role in establishing the institution's principles of academic freedom and fostering a culture of research excellence.

- J. Robert Oppenheimer (1947-1966): Renowned for his leadership in the Manhattan Project, Oppenheimer served as director during a crucial period of post-war research and scholarly growth.

- Carl Kaysen (1976-1987): Kaysen's tenure saw increased interdisciplinary collaboration and a focus on international and public policy issues.
- Edward Witten (2014-present): A prominent physicist and mathematician, Witten has continued to uphold the IAS's commitment to interdisciplinary research.

2. Interdisciplinary Collaboration:

One of the defining features of the IAS is its commitment to fostering interdisciplinary collaboration among scholars and faculty members from various fields. This approach has led to innovative research and new insights.

Scholars at the IAS are encouraged to engage in cross-disciplinary dialogues, attend seminars, and collaborate on projects that transcend traditional academic boundaries.

3. Schools and Research Programs:

The IAS is organized into several schools and research programs, each focusing on specific academic disciplines. These include the School of Mathematics, the School of Natural Sciences, the School of Historical Studies, and the School of Social Science.

These schools provide a framework for scholars to collaborate and pursue research in their respective fields while also engaging with colleagues from other disciplines.

4. Visiting Scholars and Collaborations:

The IAS frequently hosts visiting scholars, researchers, and academics from around the world. These scholars bring diverse perspectives and expertise to the Institute's scholarly community.

Collaborations with other academic institutions, both in the United States and internationally, are common. These partnerships facilitate joint research projects and further extend the reach of the IAS's intellectual contributions.

5. Public Engagement:

While primarily a research institution, the IAS occasionally hosts public lectures, conferences, and events that aim to engage the broader community in discussions about scientific and scholarly topics.

These public engagements contribute to the dissemination of knowledge and the exchange of ideas beyond the academic sphere.

6. Legacy of Academic Excellence:

The IAS's commitment to academic freedom, interdisciplinary collaboration, and fostering an environment of intellectual curiosity has contributed to its legacy of academic excellence and its reputation as a center for groundbreaking research.

The directorship and collaborative ethos at the Institute for Advanced Study have been instrumental in shaping the institution's academic culture and its contributions to various fields of study. The IAS's legacy of fostering intellectual creativity and interdisciplinary research continues to be a hallmark of its scholarly pursuits.

Chapter 8: Personal Life and Relationships

J. Robert Oppenheimer's personal life and relationships were characterized by complexity, brilliance, and the interplay between his scientific career and personal experiences.

Oppenheimer married Katherine "Kitty" Puening Harrison in 1940. Their relationship was marked by intensity and complexity. Kitty was an accomplished artist and writer, and her interests complemented Oppenheimer's scientific pursuits. However, Oppenheimer's deep dedication to his work often strained their marriage. His frequent absences due to professional commitments created challenges in their relationship.

The Oppenheimers had two children, Peter and Katherine. Oppenheimer's demanding career sometimes made it difficult for him to be present with his family, further contributing to the strains in his personal life.

Oppenheimer had a multifaceted intellectual life that extended beyond science. He was well-read in literature, spoke several languages, and often quoted from literature and poetry.

His interest in the arts was evident in his appreciation for music, painting, and literature. This artistic dimension added depth to his personality.

Oppenheimer was part of influential social and professional circles. He engaged in stimulating conversations with fellow scientists, intellectuals, and luminaries like Albert Einstein, Niels Bohr, and others. These interactions enriched his intellectual life and contributed to the exchange of ideas in both scientific and non-scientific domains.

During the 1930s, Oppenheimer was associated with left-leaning political and intellectual circles. He had acquaintances who were members of or sympathetic to communist organizations. His past associations with individuals considered politically suspect became a subject of controversy during the McCarthy Era and had a significant impact on his life.

The controversies surrounding Oppenheimer's personal and political associations played a pivotal role in his life. In 1954, his security clearance was revoked due to concerns about his associations, leading to a tumultuous period in his career and personal life.

Oppenheimer's role in the development of the atomic bomb deeply affected him on a personal and moral level. After witnessing the Trinity Test and the bombings of Hiroshima and Nagasaki, he famously quoted a line from the Bhagavad Gita: "Now I am become Death, the destroyer of worlds."

This quote reflects his profound reflection on the destructive power of nuclear weapons and their moral implications.

In his later years, Oppenheimer continued to be an advocate for responsible control of nuclear weapons and international cooperation. He maintained an active role in academia and served as the director of the Institute for Advanced Study in Princeton.

Throughout his life, his personal experiences and relationships were intertwined with his deep concerns about the consequences of his work on the atomic bomb.

J. Robert Oppenheimer's personal life and relationships were marked by the tensions and complexities arising from his scientific career, his intellectual pursuits, and the political and social dynamics of his time. His marriage, family life, and interactions with fellow scholars and intellectuals reflect the intricate tapestry of his personal experiences.

Friendships and Professional Relationships

J. Robert Oppenheimer formed numerous friendships and professional relationships throughout his life, many of which had a significant impact on his scientific career and personal experiences. Here are some notable friendships and professional relationships:

1. Albert Einstein:

Oppenheimer had a close and influential friendship with Albert Einstein. They shared a passion for physics and engaged in discussions about the implications of Einstein's theory of relativity.

Einstein's support and collaboration with Oppenheimer played a role in Oppenheimer's rise to prominence in the scientific community.

2. Niels Bohr:

Oppenheimer had a deep intellectual relationship with Niels Bohr, the pioneering physicist who made foundational contributions to quantum mechanics.

Their discussions on the interpretation of quantum mechanics and the philosophical implications of quantum theory were highly influential.

3. Enrico Fermi:

Oppenheimer collaborated with Enrico Fermi, the Italian physicist known for his work on nuclear physics and the development of the first nuclear reactor.

Fermi's experimental expertise complemented Oppenheimer's theoretical knowledge.

4. Hans Bethe:

Hans Bethe, a prominent physicist and Nobel laureate, worked closely with Oppenheimer during the Manhattan Project.

Bethe and Oppenheimer's collaboration contributed to the understanding of nuclear reactions and the development of atomic weapons.

5. Richard Feynman:

Richard Feynman, a brilliant physicist and future Nobel laureate, was a colleague of Oppenheimer at the California Institute of Technology (Caltech) after World War II.

Their interactions influenced the field of theoretical physics, and Feynman's lectures on quantum mechanics left a lasting impact on students, including Oppenheimer.

6. Colleagues at Los Alamos:

During the Manhattan Project, Oppenheimer worked closely with a team of scientists and engineers, many of whom became lifelong friends and collaborators.

Notable colleagues included John von Neumann, Edward Teller, and Richard Feynman, among others.

7. Academic Collaborators:

Oppenheimer's academic career brought him into contact with numerous collaborators and colleagues in the fields of mathematics, physics, and theoretical science. These collaborations contributed to advancements in various areas of theoretical physics.

8. Students and Mentees:

As a professor and mentor, Oppenheimer influenced and mentored numerous students who later became prominent scientists and scholars. His mentoring relationships contributed to the growth of theoretical physics and other scientific fields.

9. Oppenheimer and Kitty:

Despite the challenges in their marriage, J. Robert Oppenheimer and his wife, Kitty, had a deep intellectual and emotional connection. They shared interests in art, literature, and social issues. Kitty played a significant role in supporting Oppenheimer's work, even during times of personal struggle.

These friendships and professional relationships not only shaped Oppenheimer's scientific contributions but also provided him with intellectual stimulation, support, and collaboration throughout his career. They are a testament to the interconnectedness of the scientific community during a pivotal period in the history of science.

Chapter 9: Later Years and Legacy, Retirement and Final Years

J. Robert Oppenheimer's retirement and final years were marked by a mix of professional activities, continued advocacy for responsible nuclear policy, and personal challenges.

In 1957, Oppenheimer retired from his position as a professor at the California Institute of Technology (Caltech). His retirement came after a tumultuous period marked by the revocation of his security clearance during the McCarthy Era.

Despite his retirement from academia, Oppenheimer remained actively engaged in public discourse on issues related to nuclear weapons, arms control, and international security. He continued to advocate for responsible nuclear policy, emphasizing the need for nuclear disarmament and the prevention of nuclear proliferation.

In recognition of his scientific contributions, Oppenheimer received numerous awards and honors in his later years. Notably, he was awarded the Enrico Fermi Award by President John F. Kennedy in 1963.

Oppenheimer's health began to decline in his later years. He was diagnosed with throat cancer in 1965 and underwent treatment. His illness, coupled with the personal and professional challenges he had faced throughout his life, added to the complexity of his final years.

J. Robert Oppenheimer passed away on February 18, 1967, at the age of 62, in Princeton, New Jersey, USA. His death marked the end of a remarkable life and career that had a profound impact on science, ethics, and international security. Oppenheimer's contributions to physics, his advocacy for responsible nuclear policy, and his moral reflections on the consequences of the atomic bomb continue to be remembered and studied by scholars, scientists, and those interested in the history of science and the ethical dimensions of scientific discovery.

His death marked the end of a remarkable career that had left an indelible mark on the fields of physics and nuclear science.

In the decades following his death, historians and scholars have continued to assess Oppenheimer's role in the development of the atomic bomb, his contributions to science, and the complex ethical and political landscape in which he operated.

In conclusion, J. Robert Oppenheimer's retirement and final years were marked by his ongoing commitment to issues related to nuclear policy and international security. His influence continued to be felt in both academic and public discussions on the responsible use of nuclear technology and the moral dimensions of science.

Manufactured by Amazon.ca
Acheson, AB